ADIRONDACK

Roger Mitchell

P O E M S

BkMk Press
University of Missouri-Kansas City

ACKNOWLEDGEMENTS

I wish to thank the staff of the Adirondack Museum in Blue Mountain Lake, particularly its librarians, Vijay Nair, Jerold Pepper, and Nancy Berkowitz, for their assistance and suggestions during two long visits to the Museum's library. I also spent valuable time in the Keene Valley Public Library and in the library of the Essex County Historical Society in Elizabethtown. I would like to thank Nancy Edmonds and Dorothy Plum, respectively, for their help. Part of the reading for this book was done with the help of a Grant-in-Aid of Creative Activity from Indiana University. Large parts of the book were written during two residencies at Ragdale art colony. Let me also thank the editors of the following magazines where parts of the book first appeared: ABRAXAS, AMICUS JOURNAL, BLUELINE, CHOWDER REVIEW, HARVARD MAGAZINE, KENTUCKY POETRY REVIEW, THE MAGAZINE OF HISTORY, MID-AMERICAN REVIEW, PASSAGES NORTH, POET AND CRITIC, RIVER CITY REVIEW, and TRIQUARTERLY. Publication of this book would not have been possible without the assistance of the Adirondack Museum and Indiana University. My thanks to both institutions.

I owe special thanks to Tam Lin Neville, Herbert Stern, Emily Neville, and Judith Roman for their interest and support and to Scott Sanders for his encouragement.

R.M.
Bloomington, Indiana

Cover, book design and typography by Michael Annis/Typography

Drawings by Roger Mitchell on pages:
Title page, 10, 30, 31, 32-33, 41, 44-45, 50

Library of Congress Cataloging-in-Publication Data

Mitchell, Roger
    Adirondack.

    I. Title
PS3563.I82A66   1988   811'.54   88-14501

First paperback printing, 2003
ISBN 1-886157-44-8

for Judith

CONTENTS

Who called it Pisgah because they
saw God, and the cross on Whiteface
made it palpable. Who they were,
neither sundayschool nor teacher
cared or seemed to know or found out.

Nor have I, though I think of them.
I lived on the lower meadows
of their dream, ignorant of them.

From *Moving* (1976)

"... find out for oneself"
—Charles Olson

"I wish
I'd seen Vermont, the whole Vermont, just once ..."
—Hayden Carruth

"... imagination is not, as is sometimes thought, the ability to
invent; it is the capacity to disclose that which exists."
—John Berger

"We live in a camp."
—Wallace Stevens

"It was not for sketches that I ascended Chocorua, but for thoughts."
—Thomas Cole

"... The point is *to get all* that's been said on a given subject. And I don't
mean *books*: they stop. Because their makers are usually lazy. Or
fancy. Or they are creative. And that's the end."
—Charles Olson

"... all these phenomena are important"
—Marianne Moore

"... he will tell you history and no lies"
—Homer

"We have failed to live up to our geography."
—Theodore Roethke

HOW IT STARTS

It starts with wanting to know something,
with wanting to stop being the baffled drifter,
with being the baffled drifter, of course,
in the first place, but then wanting to stop.

It's not that I'm angry.   It's not that.
In fact, it's a nice role, the baffled drifter.
There is so much to be baffled about,
if one chooses.   And who wouldn't, or doesn't.

It starts with knowing enough already.
One can know enough already, and not
know it.   One can go on knowing and know,
at the end of it, not how to chop wood.

Or to stand still.   Sometimes I think
of standing still.   For a year. Don't worry,
it's just a thought.   But I think it anyway,
standing there thinking of standing there stone still.

NAMING

I

ADERONDACKX: Mohawk for Frenchman or Englishman,
   according to an anonymous Dutchman, 1634.
ATTIWANDARONK: Huron for the Neutral Nation,
   as recorded in the *Jesuit Relations*,
   meaning "those who speak
   a slightly different language."
RONDAXES: Mohawk for Huron.
   See Adriaen Van der Donck.
ADYRANTHAKA: Mohawk for Canadian or French Indian.
   The Reverend Johannes Megapolensis
   reported to the Classis of Amsterdam
   that the Mohawks were at war with these people, 1658.
RONDAXE,
ARUNDAKS: Iroquois words in Dutch
         and later English accounts
         of the colony of New York,
         referring to the French Indians.
ARENDAHRONON: Huron for the Rock Clan.
   "They of great rocks," or perhaps
   "They who are great rocks,"
   who lived along the lower St. Lawrence valley.
TATIRONTAKS: Mohawk for the same, except,
         not having the word "rock," they used "tree,"
         and then made them, no one knows why,
         eaters thereof,
         — AK in Mohawk meaning "to eat."
         "Those who eat trees."
         "Bark eaters."
         "Adirondacks."

II

Named by a professional geologist, Ebenezer Emmons, not of the area, hired in 1836 by the legislature of the state in which these mountains lie, at a considerable distance from the centers and avenues of commerce, to survey and catalogue its geological and mineral peculiarities so that said legislature could more knowledgably fund those who would undertake the natural and financial hazards of extracting this wealth and transporting it to those localities where it could be divided, manufactured or shaped into marketable articles.

Who felt impelled to commemorate what he thought were the original inhabitants of the area—long gone, in fact, never seen by any white person, and, as argued by some, never there—using a language he did not know and which philologists today knot their brains to know the secrets of.

And so by said half-informed gesture giving a name to what, for him and for others, had been nameless, hence useless and formless, terrifying, as matter was before the creation of it, as the Void was before the Word.

And bringing into being ways of life and habits of thought he could never have imagined, or wanted. Could Thomas Jefferson have imagined you or me? Where are the burgeoning canals, their barges sunk to the gunwales with lumber for making houses and more barges, with ore for the iron plow, bales of sheep wool for the spinning wheels of Wilmington and Philadelphia, George Caleb Bingham along for the ride, painting his jolly flatboatmen for the hundredth time, banjos and laundry flapping off the back deck?

Who put a word, it could have been any word, down? It could have been the Saint Margaret Mountains, and would have been, if Montcalm had got the better of Wolfe on the Plains of Abraham, where you can see—or nearly—on a clear day, as Cartier did in 1535, and was the first European to do so, as far as we know, his eye glancing at and then passing over those ripples of the landscape, that sea-shaped rock, of which we speak.

They might have been, as they were for a long time, the Aganuschion or Black Mountains, though John Todd thought they were blue, "those blue mountains withdrawn from the world ... where Nature walks alone," the namer of this place, this geologist, Ebenezer Emmons, having no wish to walk alone, to "peep," as John Todd did, "into the very cupboard of nature," but walked up what he then, having walked up it, and been with the first to do so, called Marcy, with a party, full force, guides and all, and named it after the governor who commissioned him, and called them all, the Adirondacks. Mohawk for Frenchman, Huron for Rock Clan, Iroquois for French Indian, Mohawk for Huron, all of them speakers of slightly different languages.

Who claimed this place by visiting it, by putting a word down next to it, which those who came after had to pronounce and live with and fill up, as a life is filled up, with itself.

As a child before it is named is anyone and no one and who when the weight of a Mary or a William is brought down and placed on it is made in shapes that are only those and never those of a Sarah or Ebenezer, the name creating the life, in ways that only the life reveals.

And so, having been named in confusion and with unrealizable hopes, but with an eagerness to be fair and to know, or if not know, acknowledge, or if not acknowledge, mention, the past, this place, acts out the life of its name and naming, in the lives of those who can no more than pass through it.

PANUGAGA

*(Pierre Radisson was captured by Mohawk Indians in the Spring of
1652 near his home in New France, now Canada, and taken to their
villages along the Mohawk River. He was eventually inducted into the
tribe as a brave. In the Fall of 1653 he escaped by running away to the
Dutch settlement at Fort Orange (Albany). From there he sailed back to
France, only to return to New France the next year and live the rest of
his life as a voyageur and trader.)*

●

This is no China, no; no rich Cathay.
You come there, and you are where no one was,
ever.
    Except those there already, they
who never saw fair skin till now,
who did not stint to make me one of them.

I slept in the long houses without fear.
I lay under the same blanket.

For I am Orinha, which means stone or lead.
As you say Peter, they say Stone to me.
Come sit by me, Stone, they say.   Which I do.

This is praise, not just to sit by them,
but to be called by stone or lead
which are great things in that country,
                                        of weight.

●

What you think bushes suddenly are not.
So with a quail calling to its mate
or a branch fallen, they who take the shape
of anything alive.   Suddenly rise up
a multitude of people from the earth.

And that is how it was with me, like that.
Everywhere around me the leaves stood back,
my two friends dead, beheaded at my feet.

●

They ran before me and behind.   I fell.
We came to water and their hidden boats.
Into the bottom I was flung, face up.
I watched the sky and listened to them breathe.

This is my life, I thought, this sky passing.
Part of it lies above my bed, unmade,
the table set for dinner, the boiled meat.
My mother, somewhere in the house, looks up.

●

            Not just a name I had,
but mother, father, brother, two sisters.
I took the place of him I never saw,
their blood son and brother who died fighting.

They combed my head.   They smeared it thick with grease.
Which you think foul, and I did too at first.
The young men taught me words, like cat and dog,
were earnest I should say them right, like them,
clapped when I did, as children clap, palms flat.

The woman, she, my mother, gave me shoes
and a blue robe, then searched my clothes for lice,
and finding them, bit them
as though they were substantial meat.

The preparations done, she came to me,
her face turned half away.
She asked if I was Asserony.   French.
No, I said. Panugaga, one of you.

It was then she called me by her dead son's name.

●

My father, nineteen scars along his thigh,
one each for a man he killed in battle,
my father, a lord or duke of that place,
fed three hundred men at once, those they call brave,
so I might walk among them with my name.

My sisters made me clean.   They greased my hair.
My mother brought a coverlet,
a cap, both red and blue, and necklaces,
two necklaces, of shell, which they call wampum.
My sisters made me bracelets of the same
and garters.   My brother rubbed my face with paint,
strapped feathers to my head with thong.

Last of all, my father, who gave me garlands,
who placed over my head a necklace, long,
the longest yet, so long it brushed my heels.
And last, into my hand, placed the hatchet.

He made a speech, one I couldn't follow,
then broke a kettle full of cagamite.
Thick meal oozed upon the ground. Next, they sang,
and young men brought down dishes heaped with meat,
and there were flowers mingled with the meat,
slabs of venison and bear,
salmon cut in foot-long slices,
and we did eat thereof, blossom, root and thigh,
until we could not rise.
                    And being done,
they turned to me and cried: Shagon, Orinha.
Shagon. Be hearty, Stone. Be hearty.
                    ●
"Chopped with swords to cut off nose and ears,
ripped out his genitals to feed the dogs
and raging hacked his hands and feet away."
So Melanthios at the hands of Odysseus,
Melanthios, already bound and tied.

I thought never to have seen such things
as I have read in books.
                    But there they were:
a man given his own cooked flesh to eat,
a woman, the child torn from her slashed womb.
                    ●
There was such thawing as made the brooks
flow like rivers. Which made us imbarque to wander
over that sweet sea, the weather lovely,
the wind fair, and nature satisfied.

Fourteen days we wandered, stomachs tight
against our backbones. Nothing stirred, no quick
scurry, no leap or sudden hammering of wings.
Then, two stags. We devoured them, dung and all,
which made all bitter. Our prisoners groaned
to see us eat. Whom then we killed.

Here we took many bears. And here
we made carriages through many stony mountains.

Two hundred beavers, trapped and taken,
some dressed so well they held the oil of bears
as pure bottles.

On our return, my mother, leaping and singing,

came to greet me. My mother, leaping
and singing. There was but banqueting thereafter,
days and nights.

●

And here I am escaped, I don't know why.
Six weeks in a Dutch ship, and three waiting
before that, the grease stink still in my hair.

My father wanders now. He will find me,
he thinks. He will bring me back. All will be
as it was and should be. I am just over
the next mountain. He can smell my camp fire.
He drives my brother and the rest toward me.
There will be rejoicing. He is sure of that.
I see him crouching in the bush, calling,
making the cry of the hurt sparrow-hawk.

●

One day I will come upon my brother.
I will not know him at first, nor he me.
He will have three small beaver pelts and the skin
of a doe found dying in the snow.
The pelts will be riddled with disease,
the skin worn. We shall look at each other,
then start to haggle, he asking the world,
me offering the customary trinket,
and when I offer him the glass of cheap rum,
he will drink it at a gulp and say nothing.
He will leave, and he will leave forever.

PEHR KALM AND LARS YUNGSTROEM: SONGS AND DANCES

(Pehr Kalm was a botanist and Professor of "Oeconomy" at the University of Abo, Sweden. He was sent by the Swedish Academy to the New World to gather information and seeds to help diversify a limited Swedish agriculture. He was allowed an assistant, Lars Yungstroem, whom he describes as "a gardener well skilled in the knowledge of plants and mechanics, who had at the same time a good hand for drawing." They left Uppsala in October 1747, spent a few months in England, and then came to the English colonies of North America. What follows is based on their journey in 1749 from the English to the French colonies, from Albany through Lake Champlain to Montreal. They were away from Sweden for several years.)

"Meeting Trees"

We met continually with trees
fallen down. We also met them
upright. We met with trees aslant,
as well, trees half way down, or more.
Though sometimes less. These,
though neither up nor down,
we also met continually.
         In Sweden, trees
are not like this. We meet, of course,
but less continually.

"Lying Awake at Night"

The air was calm and no leaf stirred.
I lay there listening, the air
calm, the leaves above me stilled.
I had never heard so little
or so much.
         Then, the sudden crack,
the swish of tearing leaves, a thump.
Like the shutting of a door
in a distant entryway.
Like a door shut for the last time.

"The Effluvia"

The effluvia toward evening
were strongest near the river banks,
and though·we poled along them, looking,
lifting the heads of strange vetches,
fescues, ferns and flowered vines,
parting the thick vegetation
with a stick, sniffing the least leaf,
we never found what caused them.
We knew what caused that other smell:
the shy, sly, gristly musk rat.

"Hymn to Lars Yungstroem, His Assistant"

Handy with axes, mechanics,
a good hand at drafting, a cook
who can conjure a meal out of
musk rat, a man who can lift,
who can sit, who can smoke a pipe.
Who can tell by feeling the leaf
what the plant is, by the plant
the depth of the root, by the root
the state of the dirt, the nature
of nature.
       Who's Swedish, to boot,
and who knows what heat and the snakes
are, and are plotting. And who smiles.

"Lars' Song of the Beaver"

The beaver bites the tree off neat.
He does it with his teeth.
He builds a dam, says here I am,
you'll find me underneath.

I like the beaver, I like his tail.
It makes a big whack.
The water combs his hair out smooth.
I'd like to take one back.

In Sweden are no beavers.
In Sweden are no dams.
All we have in Sweden is
rutabagas.

"Song of the Captured Boy"

The boy in breeches, shirt and cap
is suddenly a man.
One wonders if, at nine years old,
he'll make an Indian.

His father's head sits on a pole.
There is not much to say.
They have honored their killed brother.
It is their way.

"Lars' Song to the Huron Maiden"

O lovely Huron maiden,
you make me think of Sweden,
your skin
the color of the rutabaga.

"He Writes His Monarch
on a Delicate Subject"

As I do not know Huron well,
and, as there is no sign, or none
I could quite bring myself to make,
for the venereal disease,
thinking all the while, Your Highness,
of Sweden and of your high charge,
I regret the secret of the cure,
the root or the blossom, remains so.
There were certain smirks among the braves,
as I was broaching the subject,
quite disconcerting, as well as
odd guttural hoots and low grunts,
which I did not enquire into.
That night, one of their women, flushed,
came to me, but you may be sure
that neither I nor Lars (though not
without reminding Lars of his mother,
twice) has stained the Swedish nation.

"Now and Then"

Now and then a little river
falls. Only now and then. The sound
of water falling is the sound
I heard at birth. I heard it then,
and now, along the lake, little
rivulets of water rattle.
I'm not sure where I am. My book
is packed away, my quill is dull,
and the boat drifts.
                    Look, a fish.
Lars has hooked us dinner. Clever Lars.

KNOW YE THAT WE *

of our right forever
                    fully
and freely for a sum
of money
            absolutely
and fully
and forever
            for ourselves
and our Nation forever
at a Publick meeting
                    fully
and freely
and absolutely

●

grant, Bargain, sell,
release, convey, infeoff,
Cede, dispose of, surrender

                    forever

●

all tract & Tracts,
all parcel & parcels,
all Quantity & Quantities,

and also all
            and singular
the Trees
            and also all
the Woods
and Underwoods,

the Rivers, Streams, and Ponds,
the Creeks, Rivulets, and Brooks,
                                and Runs,
        all and each

19

●

as well as all
flowages and seepages else,
droplets of moisture,
accumulations of dew,

for which neither we
nor the drafters of this deed
can find name,

●

the land which underlies the land
and that which underlies that land,
                                    and all,
as deep as may be reached,

●

water that shall fall from the sky,
drizzle or deluge,
                    air,
motionless or not,
which shall lie on this land
        or pass across it
or cross and recross it,
                    at whatever pace,
according to its whim,
                    up
even to the furthest reach of the eye,

            and beyond,

●

the light
and the dark

and all gradations between them,
                            dusk
and dawn,

and before them and after them both,

the light at midsummer's midday,
cloudless,

midwinter's midnight,
moonless,

•

and the animals that walk thereon,
of whatever sort and variety,

the clumsy, swift-legged moose,
the remotest vole,

the beaver, the panther,
the beetle,

those that burrow,
                    however deep,
those that fly,
                    however high,
or far,

so long as they shall return,

•

all manner of thing
                    forever,
all aspect or quality,
all attribute
                    or way,
fully
          and freely,

•

          so that
in time to come
when we are asked for,
they will not know
what word to use.

•

Hendricks, alias Tayahansara   Mark.
Lourance, alias Agwiraeghje
Hans, alias Canadajaure   Mark.
Johans Crim, alias Onagoodhoge,

          we
          of the Mohock Castle

*In 1772 representatives of the Mohawk Indian tribe sold over a million acres of
land in northern New York to white land speculators for 1135 pounds "lawful
Money of New York."

REUBEN SANFORD AND JOHN RICHARDS, SURVEYORS, MAKE THEIR REPORT, OCTOBER 1827

"... where an ordinary surveyor could hardly be paid for
the exercise of his profession."
— Charles Fenno Hoffman
"... the desart place where we were." — Pehr Kalm

The most easterly line of this tract
is also on land of second quality,
the term, first, being inappropriate
to any we saw in all those weeks.
From the south east corner to the river,
it is fifty-five chains. Thence,
on very rough steep hills and high mountains,
rocky, and the passage thwarted
on all sides by fallen trees, mossed,
and of great size and age, their criss-
crossing on one another so continual
and inveterate as to be often vexatious.
This is of fourth quality, no more,
where streams and twisted brooks rush down
between the rocks and mountains,
leaving no smooth place anywhere.
One hill or mountain crowds close behind
the other all along, reaching,
at the north boundary and on rough steep hills
a high rocky spruce-bound mountain.
The land, we repeat, is of the worst kind,
but for a few small pieces to the south.
On the west, it is again rocky, broken,
though timbered with spruce, cedar, fir,
some beech and a multitude of birch.
Stupendous rocks and ledges, craggy
and irregular, in many places
kept us from running lines.   And the insects.
The locusts of Egypt were a harmonious choir
to these pestilent nuisances.

Animals of every sort abound.
It is a wilderness, no more, no less,
and will not soon cease being such.
How you will convince reasonable men
and their wives willingly to place themselves
in so barren a place, we do not know.
The isolated hunters and hermits hereabouts
do not seem suited to your purposes.
Indeed, they would be hostile to them.
The winters are unforgiving. There are no roads.
Once mined, the ore will lie on your hands.
It is our advice, though not asked for,
to abandon this scheme and seek your fortune
elsewhere. Leave this pathless waste
to the panther and the bear.

THOMAS COLE (1801 - 48)
TALKS ABOUT HIS ART

*(Cole was the most famous of the Hudson River School of painters.
Though most of his paintings were based on sketches done in the
Catskills, he visited the Adirondacks a few times and did sketches
there for one or two of his best works. His last visit was in 1846 when
he and his friend, Louis Noble, hired the services of the famous guide,
John Cheney.)*

I blame it all on Bolton and the times.
Bolton-le-Moor in northern Lancashire.
The name sounds quaint, I know, with its hints of France
and stern north country moor, but Bolton
was neither quaint nor French, not anymore.
England was at war with France, and the moor,
dissolved in smoke, lay littered with shanties
where people flung what was left of themselves
after twelve and fourteen hours at the looms.
They came from everywhere, shepherds, farmers,
all of them thrown off land they couldn't own,
land their families had worked as far back
as they could think, or farther, if the songs
they nursed their children on made any sense.

Bolton doubled every year or so,
and Bolton was only one of dozens
of country villages against a stream
in that part of England.   They needed water
for the mills.   In time, you couldn't tell
where one town ended and the next began.
It was all one smear of muck and money.

For a man of trade, an ordinary man,
who made and sold ordinary things — shirts,
brass kettles, buttons, soap — to suddenly
have ten liveried servants and a coach
and grounds you might get lost on if you wished,
with deferential groundsmen doffing caps,
and twelve-foot fences, stone laid upon stone,
a hundred miles around, for that to happen
to a man, an ordinary man,
made the land seem shabby and the air marred.

My father never wanted that, exactly,
but those who did broke him. It was a bad time.
With the war over and Napoleon
on Elba, England was victorious,
but little more. Businesses collapsed,
wages were reduced, thousands lost their jobs.
And this where you were lucky if you lived
past twenty. Riots cracked the countryside.
One ended in a massacre. Peterloo,
as it was called, was a small Waterloo
mounted against the English workingman.

Two years later, we sailed for America.
I was eighteen and eager to be free
of history and things got by getting.
It was still possible to see the world
as the world must have been, before Bolton.

I was a plain man. Nature was my balm.
I loved the grand in nature, the broad sweep,
and when nature didn't cooperate,
I put some sweep in. Once, in London,
the critics damned my things as false to nature.
But nature isn't just the view, I said.
Nature is the place where God leaned his shovel
between tasks. He leaned his forearm just there.
And you're going to rub the print right out,
I said to the man, my neighbor, who logged
the valley bare where I grazed my eyes.

They looked upon the world as theirs to use,
so I draped thought across the mountains.
This is what you see, I'd say. This tissue
of the eye. Some did. Others saw only line,
arrangement, mass. Studio jargon. No,
I'd say, that's nature you see massed, arranged.
You can't mass nothing. Something comes before.
Yes, I see, they'd say. Who knows, maybe they did.

Between utility and art shoptalk,
nature was either lumber or a flick
of bright green highlight in a mass of blue.
Were they both utilitarians,

artist and entrepreneur, using trees
for their own, not nature's, purposes?
Yes and no, I suppose. Like everything.
I finished "Course of Empire" in the year
they put the railroad through my valley.
I put them nowhere, safely out of reach.
If they were nowhere, though, I could have sketched
the first one less than ten miles from my house.
I called it "Savage State," but it was home.
I wanted everything to leap, and yet
be still. I wanted spring, at dawn, the drops
still clinging to the bursting foliage.
As though the earth had risen from the sea
just then, and shook itself, and shook again.
The deer would not be slaughtered, not today.
the druids in the distance raised their arms.
This was the world, as it was given us.
Romantic, I suppose, but still real.

The paintings in the middle must have come
from Gibbon. The whole series was a rise
and fall, in five stages. Except the fall,
to me, was not a fall, but a coming back
to the first shaken twitter and the dirt.
In the middle, splendor thick as liver paste,
people gorged inert on thick slabs of pomp,
nature like a shy beast hidden, waiting.

In Italy, I took my eye to school.
It had to look at Botticelli once,
at least, to call itself a painter's eye.
But I was ruin crazy like the rest.
I gazed at gauzy beauties for an hour.
I gazed until my eyes grew gauzy, too.
And then ran out to look at something wrecked,
neglected, crumbling, slanted toward the ground.
The others painted, leaning on a sigh.
Ah me, their paintings seemed to say. Life's short,
but here's a pretty way to die. Ho hum,
I thought. Why the gloom? Nature's coming back.
Praise the weeds for growing. They don't care.
They crack the thickest wall, dislodge the plinth
in front of which we stood in herded ranks.

The farmers fence their fields with caesar's bones
In desolation all things start, not end.
Chaos, lovely chaos, comes again.

I couldn't wait to paint it, rushed ahead
and did it out of sequence.   There, I said,
I'm headed there.   Then, I held my nose and plunged
up to my armpits in civil swill.

THE GUIDES

I. Afternoon at the Guide Museum

"not so much a lover of nature as a part of nature"
— Charles Dudley Warner

Don't let the soiled, stubby, bow-legged thrust
fool you. This one was much sought after,
subject of essays, often visited.
This other lived in a bark shack with his dogs,
hunted, — though not for the meat (which he ate),
nor for the love of uncanny skill (which he had) —
is said to have killed the last moose in the state.
This one had five children, a wife,
got "howling" drunk whenever he could.
One day he stopped, and he stopped for good.
This one wrote verses and never bathed.
This one was painted by Winslow Homer
next to this other, though neither was named.
This one was known to have beaten his wife
and was almost taken to court. This one
played violin. Not fiddle, but violin.
This one led Benedict Arnold to Canada,
this other Burgoyne toward Saratoga.
Neither appeared in the dispatches
nor was afterward blamed for the defeat.
Most of them came here from other places —
Scotland, Vermont — though this one was Indian.
That paddle he holds was his real paddle.
This one was known for his way of saying
a single word. The word was "well."
This one put John Brown's body into its grave,
where, as the song tell us, it moldered.
This one was seen once, flat on his face,
hugging a mountain. "I'm with you again,"
he was heard to whisper.

This last one, no one remembers.
He is the most popular one in the exhibit,
the one people touch. He is the one
who, in the photograph, can't be identified,
who stands off at the edge of the picture,
a saddle of venison slung like a yoke
over his shoulders and neck, who was asked
to stand still for a moment, and did,
but who couldn't, or wouldn't, look
straight into the future, at you and me,
whose name, though not for that reason,
or so we assume, has been lost or forgotten,
but whose slight, muscular body, —
not quite in focus, on cracked paper,
in a picture taken by someone else
we can't identify, almost thrown away —
shows us the unease of a man hired.
Though some prefer to see in the dropped chin,
the furtive eyes, the look of a man looked at,
seen, of a man who would rather have been —
like the animals he stalked — unseen.

One of you recognizes him perhaps,
the uncle whom no one mentioned, who knocked
on the back door late one night in a snow storm,
who handed in part of a bear, but was not
going to be asked in, and knew it, and so
stamped his feet in the doorway once and left.
Or the one you invented, the father
who spent the rest of his life looking
for the child he gave away. You see him
in every man you meet, looking for the child
you still are. The back of your mind collapses
like a rotted wall. Inside, a tiny,
mute swarm of memories writhes in the light,
slithers into the darkness.
Bent particles float through your eyesight.
You remember light bursting or water
surrounding you. On the day you knew
you were here forever, you slept that night.

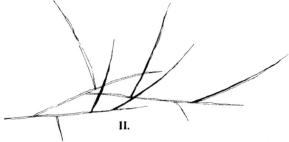

II.

"It was these people that were the routers of General Burgoyne's army. They are the most hardy, desperate men in America, the descendants of those men who fled from England when Charles II was restored. Their character is a compound of cunning and deceit. Under the cloak of religion and sanctity they will effect any object they are desirous of bringing about. They are all politicians and well acquainted with common law and the constitution of their country. Men like these are dangerous subjects."

— Joseph Hadfield, 1785

"... a more honest, cheerful, and patient class of men cannot be found the world over. Born and bred, as many of them were, in the wilderness, skilled in all the lore of woodcraft, handy with the rod, superb at the paddle, modest in demeanor and speech, honest to a proverb ... Bronzed and hardy, fearless of danger, eager to please, uncontaminated with the vicious habits of civilized life ... Among them an oath is never heard ... Vulgarity of speech ... unknown."

— William H.H. Murray, 1869

"He sits and watches every coach load of tourists and sportsmen like a hawk, and selects his victim with unerring precision. ... He has no useless book-learning or very little, but he will argue every possible question and discuss every conceivable subject. ... He is meek as Moses and patient as Job; but fights like Hector and storms like Achilles. Faithful and true, he is all your own to do and dare; but he is full of ingenious tricks, practical jokes, and long-winded stories. He takes you fishing and dumps you in the mud. ... He is the very soul of honor and can not be trusted out of your sight. ... He severely condemns city immoralities, and lives in all available concubinage. If his wife remonstrates, he turns her out of doors to follow his example. ... He is grave and truthful as a judge, and lies like Ananias and Sapphira. ... He is saving and frugal with his hard-earned wages, and gambles them away at cards."

— J.P. Lundy, 1880

"A good guide, like a good wife, is indispensable to one's success, pleasure, and peace."

— Murray

"If I were to classify such guides as are nuisances, I should place at the head of the list the "witty guide." He is forever *talking*. He inundates the camp with gab. ... The old Indian maxim, "Much talk, no hunt," I have found literally verified. ... The worst sight I ever saw in the woods ... was ... a fat, lazy lout of a guide lying on his stomach, reading a dime novel while the gentleman who hired him was building "smudges.""

— **Murray**

"Look to yourselves, ye polished gentlemen!
No city airs or arts pass current here.
Your rank is all reversed; let men of cloth
Bow to the stalwart churls in overalls:
They are the doctors of the wilderness,
and we the low-prized laymen. ..."

— **Emerson, 1858**

"... avoid an old guide as you would an old horse."

— **Murray**

III. The Paddle

There are no memoirs,
no letter or diaries,
no lists, no hand-
scrawled maps to the next
cabin or pond,
no signatures
on mortgages,
no bit of clothing,
old boot or sock,
no bottle to which once
he put his mouth,
no lock of hair,
scissor to cut with,
knife to skin bear,
gold watch or fob,
likeness of other,
tooth of the panther,
moose jaw,
lip-blackened pipe.

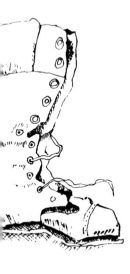

The photographs give us
the bulk of the body,
the wrinkled face.   But,
faces are everywhere.
Bodies abound.
Who has made his face
as this was made?
Who has chosen
a look, as the wood
of the right tree
was chosen, the line
of the grain?   Who
has shaved speech,
or thought, as this blade
was shaved?   Who has smoothed
the skin of the body,
darkened it
with its own oil?

This paddle, long,
squared at the end,
narrow, its handle
a T for good
gripping, a tree reduced
to a way
of being — thin,
springy, light —
of turning
as the elements
turn, in their flow,
or against them
if need be,
finding the narrow
seam in the air,
feathering
the leaden water,
the self, hidden,
though not from itself,
guiding itself, lulled,
at the world's edge
over the quick
falls, beside
the dark woods.

A TOUR, 1855

(Lady Amelia Matilda Murray, maid of honor at the court of Queen Victoria, came to North America in 1854 and spent almost two years touring. In 1856 she published Letters From the United States, Cuba and Canada. *The American edition appeared the next year. What follows is taken from a trip she and others made, mostly by water, from Saranac Lake to Booneville in September 1855. She was sixty at the time.)*

"This plateau or table is divided into two nearly equal parts by a valley, commencing at Plattsburg on Lake Champlain, extending up the Saranac River, through the Saranac lakes, then meeting the Raquette Valley, through Long and Raquette lakes, through the Fulton chain of lakes, called by their numbers ... one to eight, then down Moose River. ... It runs ... a south westerly course and a distance of ... one hundred and fifty miles, terminating near Booneville, Oneida County."
  — Farrand N. Benedict (?),
  "The Wilds of Northern New York," 1854.

•

I landed to sketch the scenery
and was so absorbed
I left my parasol in a bush.

I thought of leaving it there,
parody of wildflower,
of the hunter or trapper
years from now
passing solemnly
through the forest,
disturbed in his revery,
of its being bought at Harrod's,
adrift
in the world of nature.

But when I asked,
Mr. Moody kindly rowed back
to fetch it.
•

They are all delighted with me,
and I with them,
but it is an odd delight,
they amazed that a woman
would come here
who wasn't compelled
by birth or marriage,
and I, I suppose,
that such rough men
can be courteous.

Arnold's daughters,
near the end of our trip,
stared
helplessly,
six of them
standing in a row
against the wall
of their shanty.
They had never seen a woman
other than their mother.
The oldest was twenty.

And the old hunter,
days before,
rowing alone in a skiff,
dressed in furs,
bushy and fierce,
who called out,
"Where do
they women
come from?"

•

On the way in —
no other phrase will do —
I picked blackberries, huckleberries,
and a little red plum,
hard and tart,
which I thought would make
an excellent pudding.
Biscuit, brown sugar,
a little butter,
some water.
It did.

●

All forest fare
is common pot-luck.
Democracy of thought,
piracy of act.
No matter.
They liked lemon,
which couldn't grow there.
The tea, of course,
from India.
The fruit, theirs.
The pudding ... well,
who knows?
We were many
in that untouched place.

●

I tire of the public heartiness
expected of me.
I am introduced everywhere
as a lady of the court,
and so I must be.
But I am also fond
of my privacy,
which these woods
and these dour guides
almost allow me.

Yesterday, portaging
for a mile and a half
around Raquette Falls,
the trail almost invisible,
crossed every twenty yards or so
by huge fallen trees,
through deep bogs,
over slippery rocks,
often retracing our steps,
searching for blaze marks
on the sides of trees,
each of us carrying
some part of the load,
I felt I was somewhere
I always wanted to be.
I was inside something.
Inside, not outside.

•

The Raquette River flows
through maples, pines and tamarisks.
Crimson tints the leaves now,
blends with the dark foliage.
Tiny seedling red maples
dot the rocks and bogs.
Cardinal flower, blue gentian
and lilac aster show themselves.
I gathered berries of a Rhamnus,
saw large-leaved willows
and several species of Vaccinum.
Scarlet berries
of Cannas Canadensis
are everywhere,
also the white Partridge berry,
bright trillium seeds,
large and small wintergreen,
Gaubtheria Procumbens.
Now and then,
the starry flowers of Houstonias.
Raspberries and low blackberries
refreshed us on our way.
White and yellow Nymphaes
called "Lilypods."

•

Occasional settlements
dot the shore.
Near Long Lake
a ten-year-old boy
paddled out to meet us.
We asked him
if many people lived there.
"There is the baby," he said,
"and a few more."

•

Pans of tea, tin plates,
air-cushions,
colored plaids and felts,
sketch-book and presses,
books and maps,
a large tin case
with our store of grocery,

a basket full of biscuits,
a hammer
among bunches of berries,
tallow candles,
towels, hats, bonnets.
Still Life
With Wilderness.

●

The variety of fungi,
some, like white coral,
others, scarlet, orange,
pink, pure white,
black, drab, rose.
And bunches of that odd monotropa,
the Indian pipe,
constantly fringed our path.

●

The largest trout were boiled,
the smaller ones broiled,
with excellent potatoes,
tea-lemonade our beverage.
Afterwards, we played whist
with a not very white
pack of cards, borrowed
from one of the guides.
Slept soundly till one,
when everyone roused
as the fires were made up,
then back to sleep
till morning, no sound
all night
but rippling water
at our feet.

●

You must imagine
in all this
a continuous activity.
For all the rest and peace
we caught there,
it was always on the run.
Except at night,
we were always moving.
Even camp

was a series of unpackings
and packings, setting up
and tearing down,
cooking and washing,
the constant readying
for the next day's march.
The ten minutes or so
lying in the dark
before sleep,
the only sounds
water lapping
or a slight breathiness
in the fire,
except for them
nothing
but this immense
silence.
I felt sometimes
I had seen something
I was not meant to, was
where I should not be.
●
When it was over
and we had emerged,
weary, scratched,
our clothes torn,
ten straight hours
on the last day
trudging through bog
and tree-littered forest,
when we had said goodbye
to the guides, standing,
all of us,
in the wrenched silence,
when we were on our way
to Utica by coach,
jostled into more silence,
this place falling
into us,
like snow falling
in sleep,
two of the other passengers,
one an old man,

began speaking Welsh.
And like waking
to find the world
one took to bed
covered with snow,
I went back at once
over most of my sixty years
to stony hills
and the sea,
to Caermarthen
and Abergwilly.
I asked,
and the old man, David Owen,
said yes, he knew them,
Caermarthen
and Abergwilly.
So I pressed on,
almost afraid,
and I asked,
and yes, he said, yes,
I do,
I remember your father,
"that charity man."
He was blind, David Owen,
and he lived in a place
he had never seen,
and would die there.
At the edge
of this forest
which lay on my mind
like a late spring snowfall,
melting
as it fell,
my father flickered
for an instant.
It was late September
and a long winter
crouched
in the air.
Salt bright specks
seemed to pop out of it.

I DO NOT KNOW WHAT I DID DO

(Juliet Baker-Kellogg (1842-1931) lived all her adult life, perhaps her whole life, in the village of Minerva, Town of Minerva, Essex County, New York. She was married first to Wesley Rice, from 1864 to his death in 1873, then to William Kellogg who died the year after she did. She started a diary on January 1, 1865, and kept it, with few interruptions, for the rest of her life. This sequence, constructed from fragments of the diary, is all taken from the first 26 months and so makes reference only to her life with Wesley Rice. I do not try to present a reliable picture of the whole of her life, but instead what I imagine was a typical life for a woman of limited means in this place at this time.

Wesley and Juliet supported themselves in a variety of ways. They were, first of all, a farm family, but since the growing season was so short in the Adirondacks, Wesley did odd jobs outside the home, chiefly acting as a guide for hunters and fishermen. Juliet did some sewing for other people, but she also ran an intermittent boarding house for Wesley's clients. The Rice home seems to have been one of the early sportsmen's hostelries, typical of the early days of the Adirondacks. Not a hotel, it would most likely have been a house with an extra room or two added on. It is no surprise, given the rigors of the climate and of guiding, that Wesley Rice died in middle age of pneumonia.)

Wesley Goes Out
Wednesday, first: To day
Wesley went out.
                    Don't know when
he is coming back.

A Beautiful Morning

Friday, nineteenth:

A beautiful morning.
I do not know what I did do.

Saturday: Ironed.

Anniversary

February eighteenth: One year ago to day
     I was married, yes!
     To night, *he* — my husband,   promised
to come home
     but he has not
     yet.
I have been very busy   all day,
cleaning house
     and mixing biscuits,
and a little of everything.

Sunday, nineteenth: Reading to day
and looking for Wesley.
     But he has not come
at 8 o'clock   at night.
     Oh!
I think it is so wrong to stay
after one has promised to come
such a time.
     Nine o'clock. He has just come.
Had a letter from Rosina.

What I Did Do

Tuesday, twenty-third: Washed.
Working.

Wednesday, twenty-fourth: Baking.
Etc.

Thursday, twenty-fifth: About the same.

Friday, twenty-sixth: Ironed.
Cooked.

Saturday, twenty-seventh: Snow.

Sunday, twenty-eighth: Watched cattle.

Monday, twenty-ninth: Baked bread.

Tuesday, thirtieth: Washed.

Wednesday, thirty-first: Baked all day.

Thursday, first: Cleaned house.
All day.

The President's Death

Wednesday: Washing and cleaning,
doing chores.

Thursday, twentieth:
Made me a waist to day
like my sun bonnet.
Rainy and cold this afternoon.

Evening.
Wesley came about 8 o'clock. Told us
about the "*President's* death."

Friday, twenty-first: Rainy
and cold.
Not doing much.
Ironed.

The First Pond Lily

Monday, nineteenth, June:
Picked wool all day.

The first pond lily.

Washed Wesley

Friday, twenty-third:
Wesley went out.
Picked wool.

Saturday, twenty-fourth:
Ironed in the morning.
Judson, Jane and I went to Beaver Meadow
to bring home bear meat.

Sunday, twenty-fifth:
Wesley came home.

Monday, twenty-sixth:
Washed Wesley.

Tuesday, twenty-seventh:
Washed Wesley.

Wednesday, twenty-eighth:
Washed Wesley.

Thursday, twenty-ninth:
Washed Wesley.

Friday, thirtieth:
                    Wesley went out.

Going Out of the Woods

Monday, Third, July. Started about five o'clock to go out of
the woods took dinner to Bradley's went in evening to
Dower's went and got
                                    a new hat
                              walked up to see Charley
and Currants and baby saw Mrs. and Miss Towsley went to
bed about 12 Tuesday fourth went to picknick took dinner
with Mr. and Mrs. Evans saw the fireworks in the evening
went into the ballroom staid about two hours watching
everything Wednesday fifth took breakfast at
Warrensburgh
              (at half past ten)
                              was at Hadley in afternoon
went with Luther and picked some strawberries Mother
and Father came this evening Thursday sixth washed
this morning went down to Billy's Rosa Lurancy came in
the afternoon and Mary I went home with Rosina Friday
went visiting down to Billy's in forenoon went to Henry's
in afternoon Saturday started for Chester took dinner to
Warrensburgh got to Uncle Jake's about six o'clock Sunday
went up to Sidney Hill
              had some cherries to eat
                                    Monday
Wesley started for home I rode up to Aunt Lois's washed and
ironed just at night I went home with Philana Tuesday went
up to Bial Bates helped them pick wool all day took dinner
and tea there staid with Aunt over night Wednesday
Cousin Charles carried me to Horicon I stopped to Mr. Bells
went to cousin Joseph Coons staid to dinner and tea cousin
Sylvia came down to see me I went home and staid all night
with her Thursday went up to Uncle Elie's staid all day
Uncle and Aunt came a ways with me I came to Horicon
Went up to Uncle Jake's Jo
                    carried my satchel up

About the Same

Tuesday, twelfth, February: Warm,
                                            cloudy.
                I sewed some,   worked,
knit.
        Wednesday: Cleaned house,
worked,
                                knit
                                Thursday:
Worked,   knit some.
Friday: Ironed.
        A beautiful day.
                        Saturday:
Mopped.
                Sunday: Read most all day.
                                        Blowy,
drifting.
        Monday: Washed.
                                Three years today
since I was married.
                        Tuesday:
                About the same.

A Funny Time

Saturday, eighth:
                        Went out to a wedding.
                        Helped make the cake.
Had quite a funny time
                                in evening
putting them to bed.

47

Not Much

Friday, thirty-first:
                Not much.
Choring round.

I Wash the Poor Wether's Fleece of Wool

Wednesday, twenty-ninth, March:
        Very pleasant to day. Quite busy
        washing and breaking brows.
        Gathered six pails of sap.

Thursday, thirtieth: Rainy in the morning.
        Cleared away pleasant
in the afternoon.
              We are alone yet.
I have washed the poor wether's fleece of wool.
    (Wesley came in
      just as I am writing.)
Had a letter from Mr. B
              and also
one from my   *unknown admirer.*

Friday: Went down in the Swamp
after spout timber.

It Was Took Away
Wednesday: Sunny
                    but windy.
I washed,
but am in considerable pain.
Thursday, fourth: Morning
                    been sick all night.
Have not slept one wink.
Wesley has gone after the doctor.
                    I do not feel much
like living.   Evening he came
and Mr. Jones came with him.
                    Another night
of pain and agony.
Friday, fifth: Another
          day of pain. Oh,
          how horrible.
A night of great anguish.
                    Slept 2 hours,
that is all,
          in this whole time.
Saturday, sixth: Still
                    in pain.
In afternoon Dr. Gady came.
                    My child
born dead,   a boy,
                    a very large one.
It seemed to me
          soul and body
almost separated.
It was took away
          by main strength.

And Now It's Done

Monday, sixth: Washed.

        I don't know why
        I write this down.
     No one will read it.
     Not even me.

            When I wash

I like to write

            "Washed."

I did it,
and now it's done.

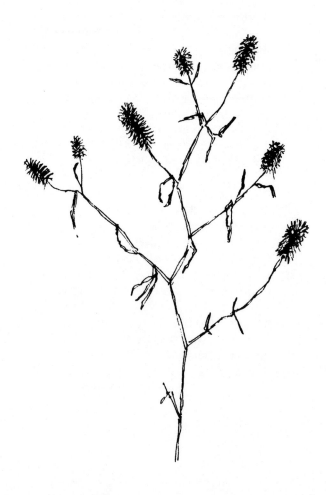

THE MONOLOGUES OF VERPLANCK COLVIN

(Verplanck Colvin was, for twenty years or more, the official surveyor of the Adirondacks; but he was, first of all, an enthusiastic mountain climber and outdoorsman. His reports to the state legislature, read at the time as much by wilderness enthusiasts as by any other group, are still among the most readable accounts of climbing and hiking anywhere.

To read the following I don't think it is necessary to know anything about surveying, but triangulation was the method used for locating a point in terms of longitude, latitude, and height above sea level. Put perhaps too simply, two known points were used to locate a third ₁unknown₁ one by making a triangle with them. Geometric and trigonometric formulas could then be used to determine distances. A theodolite was especially useful in this because it could measure angles both horizontally and vertically.)

1872
Alvah Dunning, famous guide, an old man now,
but muscular, with much life still about him,
born and bred a hunter, hermit,
skilled in woodcraft, him I chose.

Though mid-October, the sun pale, we set out.
A lumber shanty, long past use, abandoned,
we came upon, and took our first night's rest.

Deep, wet sphagnous moss carpeted our way,
held, like snow, the hoofprints of a deer, just there.

We climbed. We climbed at length a ridge, and saw
above us no more peaks.
The valleys we had left, far down, and all about it,
as far as eyes could reach, spangled with lakes.
Vegetable life recoiled, grew backwards
to its roots.   Balsam, spruce and birch were stunted.
The deep, abundant moss, a sponge swollen
with icy water, so cold our feet ached.
We clambered upon hands and knees,

had to often, were wetted to the skin,
waist high, breath visible in air,
air which chilled us though the sun,
wind-burnished, shone.

We were not there.   The land had tricked us.
We dashed along a ridge, chased
by the coming darkness, hoping not to camp
where sleep, if it took us, might not give us back.
A thick, miniature forest blocked our view.
Balsams dwindled till we stood upon an open crest.
The world seemed all below us.   We were there.

But no.   Northward, not far off, a summit reared,
grizzly with dead and withered balsams
struggling to keep their hold on bald rock.
That was Seward.   The land had no more tricks.
Between us, thick with clouds, floated an abyss.

Descending into it, we glimpsed the last
of last year's drift of snow, wretched and discolored.
Chopping our way across the valley,
the sun's last rays upon us, we made camp,
an impenetrable thicket of dwarf balsam
beside us, the true summit above us.

That night, the light shot up the northwest sky
and passing to the east made a broad belt
of crimson overhead.   The whole dome of heaven,
lit with silvery glory, flashed
and swayed in seeming concord with a gale
whose eddies then were whirling round the mountain.
With every wave and brightening of the sky,
a sighing came, as from great folds of silk.
Said Dunning, the voice of the northern lights.

Who, without coat or blanket, kept himself
alive that night, all night, by chopping wood.

Next day, at dawn, we entered a dense growth
of balsam, eight feet high at most, and pushed
or chopped, their branches stiff and numberless
and intricately locked.
                    At eight A.M.,
we walked upon the trees, dwindled
to great shrubs, flattened to the ground, with long

spreading lateral branches,
                    and stood at last
upon the summit.
                    Nowhere discernible,
as from other lofty Adirondacks,
a clearing.   Wilderness everywhere.
Lake on lake, river on river, mountain
clustered on its neighbor, numberless.

1873

An intricate network of triangles
(of points established beyond question),
each linked backward to the next, till at the end
(in one's mind) one is standing by the sea.
The sea, from which all certainty proceeds.

As thus: to take a line from each of two
known points, and where they intersect, that place,
already chosen for its geographic
prominence, whereon a flare or mirror,
thrust up by tower if need be, is placed,
that place, by geometric calculation,
angles made from the two known points to it,
becomes then known itself, stands forth, and is.
Is then no longer landmark, but fixed point,
in fixed relation to every known thing,
not just here, but where the stars stand fixed as well.

And then by process of reduction, place
this grid of fixed points on a single sheet,
as the land itself is of a single
substance made — though varied, one — and pausing,
think what one is doing, and thinking, do:

Inclose this wild and irregular area.

1898

The night we burned a mountain by mistake,
the men quivered setting their packs down.
Who had no more food, the deer startled off
by our scrambling through unbroken forest,
burdened with gear.   Vernier calipers,
rods, chains.   The delicate theodolite,
its box and harness.   Three hundred pounds
stretchered like a sultan or a sultan's
pet wife, like creamy Cleopatra, over
gorge and precipice, through swamp and windslash.

I think of that.   Of that alone, sometimes.

And the men.   I don't know why they did it,
those who did, those who didn't stalk off cursing
through the snow.   They cheered.   In the freezing gales
they cheered, when I marked and read and reread four times,
to be sure, and wrote down in the great ledger,
in a slowed hand, the last point on Marcy.
How could they not cheer?   Here, the earth unravelled,
cold, remote, treeless at its peak.   And now,
we knew its height, above Paris, London,
even the pyramids, the scuttled barge,
above her calm, wrapped body.

Undated ("I never gave a thought")

I never gave a thought to those who quit.
Captains have been set adrift before.
All wars have their deserters. Why not mine?
I fought mine against what did not seem
possible, what they said could not be done.
That they were right means nothing. To have tried,
that I will take to my grave, happily,
if there is to be one. Though to be found
lying on the floor of some hotel lobby,
mutinied by my own breath, seems more likely.

Yes, that was me muttering through the grime
of back street Albany in 1912.
I was thinking of Burgoyne's army
(another soldier set adrift near here),
of boys from Bedfordshire and Rutland.
I could almost hear the flat whack of the axe,
the crackle of falling trees, the curses,
as the road nosed forward, as the great trees
died. I think of the wormy bread and cheap rum
in the bellies of those boys, of the hope
they must have had for a quick fight, clean wound,
anything to get them on the ship back home.
Though I see one stoop and pick up a clod
of duff and crumble it through his hands.

You can still see bits of the road, or could,
logs laid out like corpses after battle.
Blaze marks, too, still visible on trees,
not many, but a few. A pile of stones
where someone thought his wanderings would end.
Dead clearings, fields gone back to forest.
Ring bolts on mountaintops, sunk in rock.

Undated   ("A thing like a map")

A thing like a map left unfinished
is always to be done.   I left my life
as I found it, here, so it would not end.
And it didn't.   It disappeared instead.
I have been studying the way things stop
recently, how there is rarely a warning,
how it has almost always happened
already, as when we wake up one morning
and, though the sun shines and it is warm, summer
is over, and also how everything
should have forewarned us, how there was death
in everything we did, long, slow strolls
through the summer dusk, and how, if a thing
can't be pure at the start, a true leap,
it can't be—can it?—at the end, an end.

UPRIGHT AND FALLEN

"There is an impassive, stolid brutality about the woods,
that has never been enough insisted on."
—Charles Dudley Warner

The featureless bland faces of Homer's boy hunters, impassive
as in watching with equanimity and disinterest the work
of their own hands, the log laid low or the hand-made knife
as its blade passes in gray light under the terrified throat,
stolid as in doing the thing doggedly, as in thinking this
is the only way, the boy-like innocence of the boy, foot cocked
on the stump, the dogs baying at the hide draped easily
over the barrel of the rifle which itself rides loosely
across the shoulder of the boy who gazes, or if not gazes,
lifts his face into the air, glazed with sunshine and sweat.

So that, without moving, as though by trick of the eye,
the boy joins the things he stands among, disappearing
among the leaping and draped forms, the upright and fallen,
blood-spattered browns, mud-shaped swales, glint and froth.
It is all one and sundered, and nothing comes back whole
but comes, if at all, like the fawn seen nibbling, quickly,
or the child full of distance it still hasn't travelled.
The gentlest wrist, blood threading its bones, is cruel,
the tree standing there and the weeds looking for light.
I have hated a stone for being there, for being a stone.

OF WILLIAM STILLMAN (1828—1901)

His life lived in the semi-pathetic way
of the post-Romantic man of leisure,
his genius dispersed, ambition blunted,
by too close a glimpse of something.
    Later travelled,

did jobwork for newspapers, the government,
turned consul in a few places,
called himself finally a journalist,
who had it in him to paint, and did,
    briefly.

One hangs in the Concord Public Library.
I have seen it only in bad reductions,
black and gray, in books, not about him,
but Emerson, who stands in the middle of it,
    looking lost and away.

Not that he gave up art.   Who wouldn't have then?
Most lit out for Europe at the first chance
or locked themselves up at home, did not come back
or out, the work assuming that flow and stoppage,
    like wrapped feet

among Chinese nobility, a badge of enviable
uselessness.   Stillman, though, is useful now,
far from the nineteenth century and the thing
he saw there which many, even the brightest,
    neglected to mention

or carried like a last meal into the ground,
bits of half-digested organic matter,
we're not sure what, maybe corn meal and water.
I speak of the woods partly, partly
    of something else.

We have here in Indiana a patch, I have seen it,
of uncut trees, original growth.   An acre or two, at best.
People drive for miles just to look at it.
Whole families, if large enough, can hug
    its biggest tree.

It is a zoo to us, a kind of gorilla
brought from another continent, as bananas are brought
to the supermarket, an invisible miracle,
as in stooping to pick up a tossed bottle we forget
        we are stooping.

Stillman went there in '54 and found what he knew
his going there would kill.   "This superb solitude,"
Emerson called it four years later, camping
with Agassiz and the rest, each with a guide,
        Stillman the host.

Who stayed on after the others left,
sent his guide back to the settlement,
one of the Martins, I think, from Saranac,
and didn't come out till November.
        And nearly not then.

The wilderness dwindles (is gone really)
under the human needs for it, Stillman
one of the last to feel there, as if by reversion,
the hush of creation, world before man.
        Which is why

this man, an American, at his life's end,
tried to make in the blunt soil of Frimley Green, Surrey,
his home of the moment, with cuttings and seeds
sent him from Albany, a thing that was now only
        inside him.

DECIDING TO GO ON

I almost miss the place, the trees and shrubs
have grown so.   And the view has disappeared.
We walk a hundred yards to see, past trees,
the mountain I had hanging in my room.

The children are quiet, polite, far away.
My wife tries hard to see me in this place.
She wants this moment for herself as well,
asks if we shouldn't knock. "They'd understand."

I turn, hearing my wishes said out loud.
The children break their silence. "Come on, Dad."
"No," I say, some sense of impropriety
too strong, a sense I must have come to here.

I make a joke instead (no one laughs),
suggest we move along.   We do.   Soon
I'm back to the old stories, their facts rubbed smooth
with telling, the faces indistinct.

Photo by Dorian Gossy

Having grown up in the Adirondacks, Roger Mitchell has written two books based on this connection, ADIRONDACK, a book of historical poems about the region, and CLEAR POND, an attempt to reconstruct the life of a pioneer millwright, Israel Johnson, who lived at the Clear Pond south of Elk Lake, a book which one critic has called "a classic of Adirondack literature." Other work of his has or will soon appear in four anthologies of Adirondack writing, including LIVING NORTH COUNTRY, ROOTED IN ROCK, THE BEST OF BLUELINE, and the forthcoming third edition of THE ADIRONDACK READER, edited by Paul Jamieson and Neal Burdick.

Mitchell is not just a regional writer, however. He has spent most of his working life in the Midwest, most recently in southern Indiana where he taught literature and creative writing at Indiana University. Aside from ADIRONDACK, he has published six other books of poetry, and a seventh, DELICATE BAIT, won the Akron Prize in Poetry and will appear in fall 2003.

Other recognition for Mitchell's writing includes the Midland Poetry Award, The John Ben Snow Award (for CLEAR POND), two fellowships each from the Indiana Arts Commission and the National Endowment for the Arts, the RIVER STYX International Poetry Award, and others. He divides his time between Jay, New York, and Bloomington, Indiana.